Write Like a Reader, Think Like the Media

Write a Media-Magnetic, Reader-Centric Book

by
Shirley A. Franklin

Copyright 2024 by Shirley A. Hammond

Writezous Publishing

All rights reserved. This book or any portion thereof may not be reproduced or used in any manner whatsoever without the express written permission of the publisher except for brief quotations in a book review.

It is our hopes that you will find useful information by going to external links. However, because of the constantly evolving nature of the internet, some of the links provided may have changed in some fashion that we could not anticipate.

Printed in the United States of America

Front cover illustration by Master Artist Ashley Dowell. Mrs.ndowell@gmail.com.

Table of Contents

1. Media Magnetic – What's It About? ... 5
2. Title Maxxx – How to Maximize on Book Titles, Chapter Titles and More ... 15
3. Elevator Pitches and Summaries ... 16
4. Your Book Signings/Your Table ... 20
5. Social Media with recommended reading of book, "Jab, Jab, Jab, Right Hook," by Gary Vayerchuk (Vaynerchuk, 2013), Self-Publishing, Giveaways ... 29
6. Getting Readers ... 37
7. Writing on Trendy Subjects ... 43
8. Video is King! ... 46
9. For the Audiobook ... 49
10. Book Covers and Book Cover Contests ... 50
11. Events, Curriculum and Books ... 57
12. Book Contests ... 61
13. Costumes, Parades & Mascots, Oh My! ... 65
14. About Amazon Author Central ... 74

15. Email List Building ... 76
16. Marketing Tools ... 78
17. Book Launch Tribe ... 88
18. Getting Reviews ... 95
19. Your Goal and Why ... 100

Media Magnetic – What's It About?

A Mediagenic book catches the attention of those who might want to do a feature story, article, segment on a blog, radio show, television segment, newspaper article and the producers/publishers of many shows/print media.

When the press shows up, it amounts to free publicity. That is why many authors tie their books to events and hold publicity stunts to which they invite the press.

I often caught people doing good, such as when I was freelancing as a reporter and saw a woman outside Wal-Mart conducting a bake sale to raise funds for her Back-to-School supply initiative. I interviewed her and wrote a feature story about her bake sale which she conducted in the hot/hot sun. She was involved in many community efforts. I wrote a second feature article about the Back-to-School supply giveaway where she gave school supplies and backpacks to needy children. I then found out that she was an author. Although I did not write about her book, I did write about her author event; Meet the Authors. Through this hours-long event, she gave authors an opportunity to meet with the public, showcase their books, read excerpts, network with other authors and sell some of their books. I wrote about this event, and then again when she launched her WOW (Woe of Writers) meeting for writers who wanted to share their thorn and rose stories about pursuing their writing passion. What I am saying, is that this woman was a media darling. While I do not suggest that you do good just to get press coverage, it does not hurt to be caught doing good. If you already have a platform where you engage in good works; let the media know about it and retain connections with them so that when your book comes out, you can invite them out to your book events.

I met another media darling when I saw a young African American female in a library showing such grace and favor to others. She was like a magnet, and I was not the only one drawn to her. I found out that she had recently finished a double Master's degree from Harvard University. Since I wrote for a community weekly that was largely distributed in the African American community, I wrote an article about her achievement. It ended up that she was writing a book which was scheduled to come out soon. She and I stayed in touch, and I ended up writing a couple of additional articles about her. One of them was about her book launch. She was mediagenic.

Some media may be trusted with an advance copy of your book, which enables them to read it and post an early review. Such reviews, if you receive them early enough, can be put on the back cover of your book and on the internet.

Watch news reports about upcoming artist interviews and take notes. Observe what kind of clothing, sitting, or standing positions, hairstyles, positioning of hands, etc. come across as open and friendly without distracting the viewers. You will want to duplicate these positives and eliminate things that do not seem to work. Whatever you wear, practice sitting and standing before a mirror so you can see if unsightliness like bulges show up. They say the camera adds ten pounds, so keep this in mind.

Listen to radio interviews; especially NPR book-based ones such as "A Way with Words." You will learn some great literary secrets this way. I would advise that you take notes.

Figure out one prop, in addition to your book, to take part in interviews. The interviewer or reporter will normally say something like; she is holding a press release, picture of____, handmade____. You should be able to tell how the prop ties into your book, or it should be obvious.

Reporters will say things like, "Coming up - Can someone change their self-perception overnight?" You may also hear something like, "Is giving a child a time-out the equivalent to playing patty cake with them?" Words like these are usually their signal to the audience that soon your segment is coming up. Perhaps they will let you help with the teaser that will help listeners and viewers stay tuned in.

Practice answering questions using words like, ("Book title here") is about rather than, "My book is about..." Listeners may wish to Google it or go to Amazon.com to look at it while you are on the air or afterwards. They may also want to buy it right away.

Be prepared to tell how you produced the title, some of the highlights and unique features and why people should care about the content of your book. Use sensory, emotional language, imagery and common terms and phrases (consider getting a free download of my complementary eBook for help in this area). Also, be prepared to explain the hallmark and extra features of your book, such as crossword puzzles, picture puzzles, Cryptograms, visual word challenges, a chapter of a forthcoming book, book tour schedules, how you arrived at a character's name, things that got edited out, etc. For instance, I offer some author trivia and an eBook with bonus material for authors – so listeners and viewers should be informed of this.

You can also blog about these tie-ins to your interview content. Wise interview subjects know how to use sound bites, which are short and appropriate bites of information/answers that can be quoted in news reports, blogs, on the air and in print. It is often extractable parts of what you have to say, usually the more promotable words. Sound bites should be easy to quote, about fifteen words long, distinctive and catch attention. You certainly want them to be memorable, like the ones you see on BrainyQuotes.com.

I have provided sound bite examples for this book below:

1. "It's time for me to share what I know after writing and self-publishing almost 30 books."

2. "This is my gift to people who don't want to spend 21 years like I did, in order to know these things."

3. "Part of my goal is to help a million first-time authors to achieve success."

4. "Books and words are right in my wheelhouse. Why not share?"

5. "My media experience is pure gold, and my avid reading experience amounts to a pearl of great price. These things fueled 'Write a Mediagenic, Reader-Centric Book.'"

6. The marketplace is flooded with books, I have captured a sure-fire strategy for rising to the top of the pile.

7. I tell others how to get media attention, readers, and reviews.

8. My goal is to help one hundred classrooms per year to self-publish a book.

If all else fails, or even if things are going well, consider having an interview (on video) to place on Facebook or other social media sites. I recently saw an excellent one with Pastor Tony Evans interviewing his daughter about her recently launched book, "She's Still There."

You can select someone of your choosing to interview you (and supply them with the questions to make their work easier and increase the likelihood that they will agree) and then video tape it and post it on social media sites. I certainly will not suggest that this is what the pastor and daughter did. I think it is highly unlikely. However, it might work for you because of the power of video.

Add success stories where people talk about their similar experiences, similar likes, and similar interests on your blog. It gives wide appeal. Many will provide such content as comments if you engage them and invite them to do so. If they comment, be sure to respond.

Add a quiz, survey, assessment, reflection section (it can engage the reader and the media). You can give the interviewer/reporter a teaser with words like, "There's a quiz to find out if you might be battering yourself without knowing it," or" I have some trivia facts about authors at the back of my book." If you have a Reader's Guide for Book Clubs, I suggest you try to squeeze that fact in during the interview.

Some people also assign activities for readers to engage in to apply what they learn in self-help books. There are plenty of authors who give something like "90 Days to Victory," "30 Days to Transform Your Business," or other end-of-book matter for their readers. Discussion questions, and reflections are also often used in non-fiction books as are study guides.

You can do practice interviews discussing answers to the quiz questions. Use catchphrases, if appropriate or if they are close to something you want to say. This will be helpful for interviews, etc. Do not forget to check out my author trivia information at the back of the book. I elected to use this in place of a quiz, but they are interesting, lesser-known facts about authors that I can discuss in interviews, on social media and on my blog, etc.

Practice using imagery to describe some of your experiences. This will be helpful for interviews, discussions, pitches, etc. The best way to get invited back by the same show host, and to gain new interview/appearance requests is to do well each time. This means you should be articulate, engaging, polite, show a positive spirit, and project great energy. Because of the possibilities here, you owe it to yourself to practice, practice, practice. If you have no one to practice with, practice in a mirror.

Have a built-in audience. Let people know that you are writing a book and get a following. This will create the demand in advance.

If applicable, advertise a profile in your company's newsletter, on corporate blogs, alumni magazines, and websites, etc. If the personnel in charge of this newsletter or other media are busy and disinterested, it could be that giving them a finished Q&A or video and video transcript might tip the odds in your favor. A summary of your book with your profile or biography (as opposed to having them ask questions that you answer for them or schedule to meet with you) will give them no excuse to turn you down.

Position content creatively in order to get people to think of their similar experiences. Doing so will help you to make connections with them. More information about generating a built-in audience follows.

Consider putting together a digital media kit that can be shared through emails and otherwise online. Many people use an infographic style, where pictures and text provide the main points worth sharing. Once you have it perfected, put it in PDF form.

Some of the features to include are listed below:

- ✓ Author profile, Artist statement or biography
- ✓ Book summary
- ✓ Author Q&A (you can recycle this for more than one purpose)
- ✓ Awards/Reviews
- ✓ Video links
- ✓ Pictures
- ✓ Information on booking you as a speaker
- ✓ A press release

Write a press release about your book launch and leave the date and location blank until time to actually release it. Press releases cannot be underestimated in terms of their power to move the hearts of media professionals.

Figure out which local media you will futuristically send the press release to. List all of their information, such as contact name, preferred means for sending, requirements and limitations (for example some allow no URL or a limited number of them). Press releases announce to media that something newsworthy is about to happen. If you write it well enough, or have it written by someone experienced at doing so; it could result in having the media attend your event, contact you for a visit at your book signing, write an article, or run a story segment on the news or radio.

When I worked as a reporter, I often decided to cover an event or interview a person because the newspaper received a well-written press release. In addition, my publishers often assigned me stories upon which to follow-up because they had read a press release that made an event or person seem interesting.

I believe other reporters, journalists, show hosts, print media publishers, podcasters and others react similarly to well-written press releases and other pitches.

Please see this list of potential reasons for writing and distributing a press release:

- ✓ Starting a new business
- ✓ Introducing a new product

- ✓ Offering an article series for publishing
- ✓ Opening up branch or satellite offices
- ✓ Receiving an award (Newberry or other honor for your book)
- ✓ Announcing that you are available to speak on particular subjects of interest (this is excellent for authors trying to get exposure. Some speak for free and ask to bring books to sell, but some accept an honorarium and ask to sell their books)
- ✓ Issuing a statement of position regarding a local, regional, or national issue
- ✓ Announcing a public appearance on television, radio or in person (an opportunity to tell others about your book)
- ✓ Launching a website
- ✓ Announcing free information available (your free eBook that accompanies/complements your print book)
- ✓ Announcing that you have reached a major milestone
- ✓ Obtaining a new, significant customer
- ✓ Establishing a unique vendor agreement (getting a book deal)
- ✓ Meeting some kind of unusual challenge or rising above adversity
- ✓ Restructuring your business or its business model
- ✓ Setting up a customer advisory group

- ✓ Announcing that an individual in your business has been named to serve in a leadership position in a community, professional or charitable organization (i.e. Your board of directors)
- ✓ Sponsoring a workshop or seminar

I obtained this information from the following Entrepreneur.com link:

https://www.google.com/amp/s/www.entrepreneur.com/amphtml/46476

As a reporter, I always had my ear to the ground and hung around libraries, bookstores, and coffee shops to hear about emerging authors. I would also follow social media, crowd-funding campaigns for books and book printing and others book-related feeds in order to cover authors and book stories.

In addition, through my book consultancy services, I have written a host of press releases for authors of all types of books. A number of them have reported to me remarkably successful outcomes, such as high traffic at their book events. This is especially true when they had me handle press release distribution for them. When I have added this service, I always sent the release to local media and to online press release sites.

Title Maxxx – How to Maximize on Book Titles, Chapter Titles and More

Catch attention and get ready for maximized results by doing the following things:

Use an attention-getting title - one that distinguishes. You also need catchy titles for your blog posts, brochures, banners, etc.

Think about adding a straightforward subtitle if you want one, and it applies and shed some more illumination on your book.

Use compelling chapter titles in your table of contents. Remember that you can also do subtitles if you have a toss-up situation where two chapter titles seem equally great or where further clarification is needed. Just do not overdo it and have too many chapters with subtitles to accompany the titles.

One extra thing you can consider is using some high-ranking keywords to help you with your title content here (and other digital content – things that will be on the internet). I use SEMrush.com to help me find the best keywords, the most popular search words. There is a little more work involved, but with this as a starting point, you can also use a print or online Thesaurus to find synonyms. You can then look up which of your chosen words in that synonym list ranks higher per SEMrush.

Elevator Pitches and Summaries

༄

Write an elevator pitch about the book. It should be short enough to deliver during a short elevator ride. Practice it with people. During any interviews, you may have enough time to provide this pitch, a little about yourself and then talk about any bonus materials that you include.

Author a book summary. Do some research online, at libraries and at bookstores to see what high quality summaries look like. Duplicate some of the features in your summary. Some authors have one summary on the back of their book, and a variation of it on the internet where their books are featured, such as Amazon.com.

Take a look at an example of an attention-capturing pitch, and back-cover book summaries, and italicized explanations as to why they are deemed exceptional:

1. Everything in life is an invention. If you choose to look at your life in a new way, then suddenly your problems will fade away. One of the best ways to do this is to focus on the possibilities surrounding you in any situation rather than slipping into the default mode of measuring and comparing your life to others. The Art of Possibility by Rosamund Zander and Benja-

min Zander, Viking Press, 2002. *This summary is succinct and whets the appetite, no wonder it is a bestseller. It gives no spoilers but teases and evokes excitement with just enough details to make someone want to read more.*

2. A Book of Literary Fiction + Poetic, Melodic and Lyrical Beauty A fully engaging book that is chock full of creativity and shot through with poetic and musical interludes, "Xtreme Ride Wish: An Untwinnable Day," will be one of this year's most widely read and most beloved block buster books. While reading this delightful title, readers get a window into Gavin's thoughts, heart and wishes; plus, the secret longings of many who show up at the city's amusement park on the untwinnable day in order to make a reversal plea. Xtreme Rides are those roller coasters with loops, twists, and other courage-challenging features. Untwinnable Day means that the day is unlike any other and can't be repeated or duplicated. This book represents a sequel to The Magnificent, Marvelous Ferris Wheel Daze, a short story which front-lines the 5-star review book Christmas Plus: Delightful. As the story continues in this new book, Gavin and a wonderful cast of characters are at the theme park, hoping to capture the blessings of the single day of phenomenal good fortune. "Xtreme Ride Wish: An Untwinnable Day," Shirley A. Hammond, Writezous Publishing, 2014. *Although this summary is overlong, it still has excellent features. It would qualify as a book description more than a book summary. It would not fit on the back cover of a book either but would work well on the internet.*

3. After getting kicked out of boarding school, Holden Caulfield is set adrift. In this stream-of-conscious narration, readers come along with Holden as he searches for connection and authenticity in New York City. *This summary is noticeably short, yet it has all the relevant details. The reader comes to know the writing method (narration that has a continuous flow where readers can know what the character thinks, and reacts to what is taking place), character details and setting, which are all crucial elements that influence readers to pick a book or pass it up.* The Catcher in the Rye, J.D. Salinger, Little Brown & Company, 1951. *This classic book has over two million ratings and almost 45,000 reviews; according to Goodreads. According to Wikipedia, around one million copies of Catcher in the Rye are sold on a yearly basis.*

In addition, here is the summary that I wrote for the book you are reading right now. It may have changed by the time I had the book cover design, but here you go:

4. "Write Like a Reader, Think Like the Media:" How to Become a Media Darling and Attract Readers

You can win the war on book marketing supremacy. Some of the key things you need are the media on your side and readers ready to read and review your book.

In this book, you will get valuable insight into how to get these two key populations on your side. Shirley A. Hammond, author, and self-publisher of almost forty books of her own, offers 28 years of accumulated knowledge about winning a good market share of readers for your book. Her degrees in Journalism and Communications; along with her many years working as a reporter, has given her keen insight into how an author can become a media darling. As an avid reader with a voracious appetite, she knows what gives certain books an advantage.

Those wells of knowledge make up the content of this book. There is also bonus material, like lesser-known trivia about authors, winning ideas she is successfully implemented, nuggets others have dropped and content she included in the college creative writing course she taught for several semesters in the Dallas area.

Your Book Signings/Your Table

Check out local bookstores and figure out which one you will use to launch your book (have your first book signing). Develop a relationship with the people there over time and get to know the layout of the store. For this second part, a customer may treat you like a worker and say, "Where are the greeting cards?" You want to be able to show them or walk them to it. This could be your chance to pitch your book and be helpful. Maybe they are getting a card for an occasion which would warrant an autographed book. Also, you have unburdened the workers, and they may tell other customers about you and let you post something about your presence there at the registers. They may also post an announcement on social media in advance of your event.

Look up Book Festivals and Book Fairs in your area and mark them on your calendar. In Texas, I love the widely attended Texas Book Festival in Austin. Other cities have book festivals, as well. Some of them are designed for a special audience, such as teen or children's books. Do your research, you may find one or more near you that covers your special genre of book, such as mystery, fantasy fiction, young adult fiction, etc. Dallas, where I presently live, has the Dallas Book Festival; DeSoto has The Great Southwest Bookfest; Irving and Denton both have

The North Texas Teen Book Festival; Austin has The African American Book Festival and The Texas Book Festival; Houston has the week-long Bayou Book Festival, Tweens Read, The Bookworm Festival and The Houston Indiepalooza. You can look up book festivals by state, or by visiting www.bookfestivals.com/list for nationwide festivals.

If you want to be a featured festival author, it is possible. Most festivals will require that you have a publicist that coordinates this for you. As there are exceptions and stipulations, be sure to check the website of any festival that you are considering.

Visit Half-Price Books (several locations) and ask about having a book event there. They are often happy to feature local authors at least once a year per book and per location. They do not ask for a share of proceeds. Most bookstores do – often it is at a 60/40 split, with you getting the larger share. Chain bookstores will also ring up all purchases of your book at their registers. When the venue rings up your purchases, be sure to keep track of sales by making tally marks for each book that a buyer takes to the register. In addition, request that they pay for the books before you sign them.

Go to your App Store and download the Indie Book Store Guide apps and search for independent bookstore websites because you do not want to overlook independent bookstores during your book tour.

See iPhone link here: https://itunes.apple.com/us/app/indie-book-store-finder/id443607557?mt=8

Here is another site where you can find stores: https://www.indiebound.org/indie-bookstore-finder

Here is one where you can find stores and download books in the cloud using Android and Apple phones: http://indiereader.com/app/

Austin has an excellent independent bookstore called BookPeople that is extraordinarily successful. I have personally seen people like Fabio, Jessica Alba, and others there. They even had Associate Supreme Court Justice Sonia Sotomayor there when her book, "My Beloved World," came out.

Do not overlook neighborhood barber and beauty shops. If you seek out the owner or manager, they may let you schedule to come in and sell at a later date. Some authors find favor by just quickly visiting on a busy day like a Saturday or the weekend before back-to-school and asking to pitch their book to customers.

At Half Price Books, you will process your own book sales. You should have change, and a means to take debit and credit payments. Some authors like Square, which you can link to your bank account and then download the app onto your smartphone. You can connect the square to your smartphone at the audio portal. The regular Square for swiping only, is free online. However, some retailers like Office Depot carry them as well. They typically retail for $10 if you do not want to wait for one to arrive in the mail. If you have an Android phone, the Square will connect directly into the phone, but you need the adaptor that comes with iPhone if you want to connect the Square and take debit/credit payments using an iPhone.

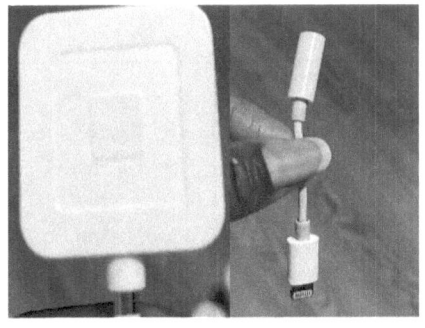

See images of my Square with the adapter attachment for iPhones. When I use this with the Square app and an internet connection, I can swipe a customer's credit/debit card, have them sign it and indicate their receipt preferences.

If you want to be able to use/process chip cards with your Square, it sometimes requires that you buy the special chip-enabled Square reader. Some people have reported to me that they obtained theirs for free by signing up for a PayPal account, others by obtaining QuickBooks. If you elect to forego this expense or addition and swipe a chip card, the bank will charge more for processing the transactions. This could potentially eat up your profits.

Make sure that you have the means for people to provide their email addresses. You can also get their social media information when they visit your table; especially if they make a purchase. Do not do it through Square nor expect the app to capture emails. Instead, create a table or spreadsheet where you have language advising them that, by providing this information, they are giving you permission to contact them. Of course, you will want a few working pens and a clipboard or firm surface for this purpose.

Write Like a Reader, Think Like the Media

See example here:

Name	Email Address	Facebook and/or Instagram Handle	Twitter Handle and/or Instagram Handle	Reading Websites Where You Are Active (Goodreads, Go-Read, Jacketflap, Author's Den, Smashwords

A short disclaimer with similar language to that provided below should accompany your email list form:

By providing this information, you agree to allow Writezous Publishing to send you information by email and social media.

I would suggest that you let them dictate how often and what type of content they welcome, as well.

Ann Voskamp has two buttons that give options for people who sign up for her emails. One is for those who want to receive her daily messages and the other is for her weekend bundle. People have to select an option and then input their email address in order to subscribe. One great nugget that this author offers to email subscribers is a gallery of downloadable frames with quotes which tie-in to her book.

If anyone at any time asks you to remove them from your list or to unsubscribe – please do so immediately and completely.

If they provide social media handles and book-related sites where they are active, be sure to reach out to them within a week on every one of those sites. You can remind them where you met or send actual pictures. Some authors even take pictures with those who visit their tables. If you post those with your contact, they are more likely to repost, share and like the post.

Although I am not a Jehovah's Witness, I liked their table, as set up in a local library once when I was at the library.

In addition to the wonderful smiles on their faces and the favorable placement near the entrance, I liked the following things:

1. The vertical side display to the right of their table. It made the display more visible.

2. Their clean white tablecloth

3. Their video screen with noticeable activity (movement). This draws attention.

4. Their branded sign on the left side of the table

5. The fact that they had books, business cards and promotional matter (brochures) on the table

6. The fact that the tablecloth reached to the floor. This might be handy for ladies with dresses.

The only thing I would have changed, and I told them when they asked my opinion, was that I would have had several of the books on a vertical display of some sort. Books should not lay flat on a table, because people cannot see them until they are up close. You want to use your craftily designed book cover to draw people over to the table from a distance. If you do not have a display or easel where you can place a few books upright, another option is to stack several books high with the spine facing the outside. People can see the title and your name (if that is on the spine) from a distance. This also makes for excellent photo shoots, because it is not just books at the table, but book titles which people can see clearly and read easily because they are elevated. At another table location the books can be stacked together where the title faces outward, which people can use to do an internet search.

When holding one of your books for a picture or stacking them for a picture – make sure your hand or hands do not cover the title and author name. That picture could show up anywhere, and may spark someone to look it up, and purchase a copy.

Regarding vertical displays, some stores may loan a few easels to you. You may also ask school librarians to save you 2-3 of them after their Scholastic Book Festivals are over. I have had several donated by a Family Christian Store that was closing, and I've had school librarians give me a few (you just want to cover up the Scholastic information, if you want – but it's no big deal because your book cover will likely cover up this information). I once had a minister at an event where I was presenting to take a Scholastic book festival triangular display as a model and he made another on-the-spot easel for me out of cardboard. This was a bonus for me because I did not feel that I had enough books sitting upright at my table.

You can also go online or find retail, wholesale, or supply stores where they are available for sale.

In closing this topic, I want to point out that not every book has to be on a vertical display. You can spread or fan out some copies on the table, in addition to displaying anywhere from 3-6 (or more) vertically.

By all means, make sure to have plenty of attractive business cards to hand out during book events and networking events. Give them out generously.

Social Media with recommended reading of book, "Jab, Jab, Jab, Right Hook," by Gary Vayerchuk (Vaynerchuk, 2013), Self-Publishing, Giveaways

One huge advantage of self-publishing is that you have more creative control over your contents, title, pictures, summaries, cover, etc. Often publishers will want you to change things. When you self-publish, you decide what you want to keep, and what you want to change. You may find this freedom ideal.

Get to know Kindle Direct Publishing by reading their website information about self-Publishing. Watch some of their videos about self-publishing. You can go the D-I-Y route with them, or look for experienced, well-reviewed talent on Fiverr.com who can convert files, download your eBook, and print book version on CreateSpace for you. I have not used them to self-publish a book, but I intend to do so soon, and I highly recommend that you at least consider them.

I also recommend Ingram Sparks, an arm of Ingram Book Company, the world's largest book wholesale distributor to bookstores and distributing companies. This is a bonus because some stores only order from book distributors like Spring Arbor. To explain the book distributor role, they are your pitch people. Marketing focused, they pitch the books in their catalog and direct sell to libraries, schools, bookstores, retailers, sales representatives in the field.

Baker & Taylor, who I have personally never used, is a wholesale distributor to libraries, schools and more. It might be worth your time to do due diligence and conduct some research on them.

Also, something I have never done is use an agent. Typically, they can help you get broader distribution. In fact, some entities in the industry will not deal directly with an agent but require that only agents inquire or deal with them.

Contact IUniverse, Christian Book Publishing and Xulon and check out their self-publishing packages. While there are a plethora of other print-on-demand, hybrid, or self-publishing companies out there, these are the ones that I know about. I also like Ingram Sparks very much, but I have not completed my process with them. I had an auto accident when I was about 85% finished getting my book up and running with them. I wanted to try them out because they do both book printing and wide distributing. I do know someone else who held a Kickstarter campaign to raise money for her book and then used Ingram Sparks to print and distribute them. Consider checking out this Tennessee-based company.

Request a publishing guide from one of these companies and read it when you get it. Often you can download it directly from their site and have it in real-time. You already know that you should read the guide and get more familiar with the self-publishing process.

With self-publishing, the print-on-demand concepts enable such companies to print as few as one copy of a book to a million copies or more. They print according to demand, or per order. If you elect to purchase quantities of your book for events and promotions, you can do so at wholesale price and sell them at retail price. Often your discount percentage increases at certain increments due to what is referred to as economy of scale.

I self-published seven titles under IUniverse.com under the name Shirley A. Franklin during the years spanning 2008-2010. Around that time, "Still Alice," was self-published through IUniverse. It did so well as a self-published book, that a publisher offered a book deal to the author. A few years later, she got a movie deal. "Still Alice," is now available as a DVD.

Consider reading the book, "Jab, Jab, Jab, Right Hook," or at least the parts about Facebook and any social media sites where you have a presence. Use that knowledge to post information about your book on social media. Two excellent take-aways that I got from the book were the importance of quality storytelling that connects you to people, and that you want to have three non-call to action posts for every one call to action posts. I learned how to like, share, and comment often to the same audience.

Facebook: Some people are not aware that some posts will be posted more than once, as Facebook allows this liberty. For example, we may share a meme with a video link where people can sign up for your emails (an explanation of how to do this will be included), subscribe to your video channel in the morning, share only the link in the afternoon, and then embed the link in a blog post in the evening.

Many authors develop and grow Facebook Fan Pages. This is one way to brand yourself as an author and potentially gain readers.

Facebook also has a Pages section such as my example below. This is a place where you, as an author, can profile yourself. I love the extra features, such as buttons and other customizable things.

There is an author and marketing expert who answers marketing questions for free. His name is Scott Hughes. He also has a website, Onlinebookclub.com, with almost a quarter of a million members. If you comment on his Facebook page, you can ask him marketing questions and he will respond free of charge, This is a winning way to serve people, and to increase your social media traffic. Perhaps you can duplicate this if you are a SME.

Instagram: Some people may not be aware that Instagram has a book-centric arm titled #Bookstagram. Be sure to check it out and see if it fits with your book promotion scheme.

Also, you can download an Instagram photo frame for people to stand behind and take pictures. You can use them at book-signing events and other events related to your book. Either you or they should post those pictures to social media with the best hashtag messages you can think of based on your Search Engine Optimization research, as explained in another chapter.

Instagram Live is growing in popularity. This might be an excellent promotional opportunity for you. Some people tape a cellphone in video mode on a wall and then record their video event. Others may have more advanced equipment.

Keep adding content like books you like and book reviews and inviting/messaging friends on Goodreads, Smashwords, Jacketflap and GoRead. For Goodreads, I also suggest that you review and rate books that you read on this site and post your book when it is available. They also have contests on there where you can give away a certain number of books. If you can get people on sites like Goodreads, where they have profiles, to add their picture to their review of your book, it gives their reviews more credibility. Screen names can also help, so be sure to add such specifications.

When it comes to Goodreads, I have run book giveaways a few times and gained more buzz and hype for my books. They have this option on the dropdown menu. All you have to do is fill out the different parameters of information (including that winning book summary) and then set a duration for your contest. You can then notify people who've you have friended about the contest and Goodreads will send out this information. People enter to be winners of whichever designated quantity of books you decide to give away. Goodreads will notify you of the winner(s) and give you the address where you are to send the book(s). They request two things of you at this juncture:

1. Send only the book, with no marketing materials!
2. Notify them when you have sent the books (at your expense).

Do not worry about the fact that you cannot send marketing materials to these winners, they are required to post reviews of your book in exchange for those free copies, and that should be enough. They are required, here and elsewhere, to include language in their review that indicates that they received the book for free. In addition, all those who did not win may elect to purchase the book or tell someone else about it. This giveaway option is a win-win. Just be certain that you select the quantity you will give away based upon your budget for this, including postage and envelopes.

Another site where you can host a book giveaway is Rafflecopter. You might consider using them as an additional book giveaway source to augment your Goodreads and other giveaways.

Run Your Next Giveaway with Rafflecopter :)

```
Run Your Next Giveaway with
Rafflecopter :)

Rafflecopter is the world's easiest
way to run a giveaway online. Sign up
for free!
```

Here is the link to an excellent informative article on properly setting up a Rafflecopter giveaway.

https://www.rafflecopter.com/how-to-enter-a-giveaway

Note: You can also run a Facebook Flash giveaway on Rafflecopter using your timeline. See more information at this link:

http://fbflash.rafflecopter.com/

AuthorsDen is another excellent place to interact with readers and other writers, and to post content. For example, if your self-help or fiction book has poems, you can submit just the poems, one-at-a-time over a period of time, to AuthorsDen and reference the book and link information in your post.

There's also BookPub, and the potential found in connecting with an influencer on social media (or on Fiverr.com who does promotions). The influencer can blast your videos, posts, weblink or other information to hundreds of thousands of people (or more) that they already have in their pipeline.

Your biography or biographies on all these sites should put you in the best possible light. You should include some high-ranking keywords, some of your best moments as relates to your life, and truthful things that make you stand out. For instance, if something like the accomplishment on the following list applies to you, include it in your bio:

- ✓ I graduated summa cum laude
- ✓ I have a non-profit for the homeless (this applies to me)
- ✓ I wrote the best paper (dissertation, thesis, essay) on the subject of raising musically gifted children
- ✓ I figured out three ways to make a D-I-Y fidget spinner for under $2
- ✓ I received double Master's degrees from Harvard University

In addition to your accomplishments, there are other things that people may want to know about if it ties in with your book, or sheds light on you as a person/author. Here are a few examples:

- ✓ I would love for my high-level copyrighted curriculum to be taught in schools around the world (this is my goal)

- ✓ I want to lead a half-million homeless people to Jesus Christ for salvation and discipleship, and to help them secure permanent housing (this is one of my goals through my non-profit Foxes Have Holes)

Do not forget to check out SEMrush.com, which I mention in the first section on mediagenic books. It will help you find higher ranking words to include in your digital biography. Do not forget to add your email address at the end of your biography and on any About the Author content.

GETTING READERS

Readers are everywhere! Your goal is to get them to read YOUR book. There are several ways to accomplish this goal, and many have been covered in other chapters. So, if you find yourself disappointed in the size of this chapter, keep in mind that it is to be used in conjunction with the other chapters in this book, and with content in my complementary eBook (not the eBook version of this book, but a separate eBook), along with videos and supplemental material that I will be providing. If you ever go after a book deal, amongst other things, the publisher will want to know what your affiliate groups are. This could include any of the people with whom you associate who could become potential purchasers/readers of your book because they have some type of inside relationship with you. So, think of yourself as an author and self-publisher, and think along the same lines as publishers. You want to identify your affiliate groups. Outside of social media your affiliate groups could be any of the following, and more:

1. Church choirs and other choirs where you currently are or previously were an active member

2. Sororities or fraternities

3. Alumnus organizations or chapters

4. Golfing clubs
5. Bridge clubs
6. Dance groups, studios, teams
7. Your own business, non-profit or business network
8. Yoga, health and fitness groups or clubs
9. Barber or beauty shop friends
10. Speech, speaking, debate and similar clubs and teams
11. Neighborhood clubs, watch groups and associations
12. Professional clubs related to your profession
13. Vegetarian, vegan, and other foodie clubs
14. Lifestyle clubs
15. Adventure, high-risk, thrill-seeking, and extreme sports groups
16. Gaming, online, digital media clubs
17. Recycling, environmental, green initiative clubs, groups and organizations
18. Benevolent, ministry, community service clubs, groups
19. Rotary, Elks, Masons, Eastern Star and similar organizations
20. Church organizations and ecumenical groups
21. Places where you volunteer

22. Places where you visit to serve and comfort others (hospitals, nursing homes, etc.). This does not suggest that your book buyers would be the people who you serve or to whom you show care and concern, but the nurses, staff, other medical personnel and various others may be interested to know that you are working on, and then have finished your book.

Even if you annually attend a specific conference, or your family has a yearly family reunion; these are considered affiliates for purposes of promoting your book. If it is time for a high school reunion, you should also use this opportunity to promote your book, gain social media followers, supporters and influencers.

It is an excellent idea to stop after you finish this section of the chapter and write down all your current and recent affiliates. After you finish reading this book, go back to the list and next to each group, write down the manner which you believe will be most effective in sharing information on your book while you are working on it, and then later when it is published. Bulletins, verbal announcements, through social media and on bulletin boards and newsletters would be some of your choices.

Hopefully, if you play your cards right, you can get the individuals who are part of your affiliate groups on your email list. Ask the president or group leader/owner. You will be no worse off if they say no, and much better off if they say yes.

Find book clubs in your area and visit a few over time. Tell them about your forthcoming book (not at the first visit unless you know some of the members and feel comfortable) and see if they will put you on their

2018 list (or your list for the following year). Your elevator pitch will really help you here.

I would suggest that you even look at getting your book added to the Mayor's Book Club; if your book is a children's book that promotes the development/enhancement of reading skills. If you have some content that aligns with the reading standards in your state, this would be a bonus worth shouting about. You can find your state standards on the Department of Education website in your state. I happen to be blessed by God to have a Master's degree in Education, and to have taught Reading for several years in the Dallas/Fort Worth area. As such, I have often added certain reading objectives within my book. Usually I embed them, rather than making them didactic.

For example, my book, "Emma's Fantastique Word Play," includes a wealth of synonyms, similes, metaphors, onomatopoeias, reading context clues/scenarios and figurative language use that helps readers with vocabulary development and to gain familiarity with several literary devices.

The same librarian that I talked to about book reviews and getting books acquired by libraries stated that the city's acquisition department selects books for the Mayor's Summer Reading Club based upon those that show high readership before the summer. So, I would suggest that if you want to be on the reading club list, that you heavily promote your book to children in your target market, so those readership numbers are high while school is in session. This is a way to double dip – you write the book and get lots of kid readers during the other three seasons (Fall, Winter, Spring), and then you make the cut for this list and children who sign up for the Mayor's Summer Reading Club will see your book featured as a possible selection! That will equal more readers, and more exposure/buzz/hype!

Also, consider adding a Reader's Guide at the back of the book, whether it is a children's book or not. Book clubs love this kind of bonus material found in the back of books. Keep in mind that many libraries and bookstores run book clubs or allow others to hold them in their space. If you cannot find a suitable one, start one of your own, using your own book to kick-start it.

Check out Reader's guides in a few books so you know what to include, what questions they tend to use. Here is where your knowledge of imagery and figurative language will pay off. You will notice that, for fiction books in particular, they typically have at least a couple of questions dealing with things like imagery, figurative language, and foreshadowing.

When the book comes out, meet with the book clubs with which you feel you made a positive connection and talk to them about purchasing copies directly from you at a discount. Be sure your discount is not so low that you cannot make a profit. This is something they will want to do anyway if their book is added to their featured books to include for the year. If they prefer to order online, be gracious and accept that. Either way, you are selling books and getting exposure. If they agree, ask them to send you a video clip from the meeting where they discuss your book (ask them to make sure the image shows your books, faces and the table where they are sitting), or at least a still image with the same request. You can then post it to social media, your blog (or blog posts to other people's blogs, along with excerpts from your book), your website and other places. If one of them wants to do a video review, that would be a bonus. See more about this later when I write about reviews.

If one or some of them want to make videos or take still pictures and post them to their social media sites, that is definitely a bonus. Be sure to ask. If they do this, make sure you repost, like, share and comment.

Careful pricing, especially for eBooks, can usually help you get readers in high volume. You have probably seen .99 cents eBooks, which are shown to help with this objective. The good news is that you can always increase the price after a special promotion.

WRITING ON TRENDY SUBJECTS

Do not be afraid to seek out podcasters that cover content or subjects similar to your book topic. Writers who write on popular subjects already being addressed usually do better than authors who do not. For example, authors who write about bullying, something on a lot of people's minds, something that is widely covered by the news, will rack up a good volume of sales. This is especially true if the book is well-written, has an excellent summary, is housed in a winning cover design, and has keyword density (more about that in the next section) in all the digital content available about the book (i.e., online book summary, video descriptions, author biography, etc.).

You can also Google or otherwise engage in an online search using the search words "Trending Subjects." You may find certain ones which have been enduring the way bullying has been or certain popular evergreen subjects (year-round, year-after-year). Those may be excellent ones to write a book about. Do not put too much hope in writing a book on a short-term trendy subject because it takes time to write a book, and people may not be interested in the subject any longer because something else is trending in its place.

When I write a fiction book, I give my characters names that are popular, according to search engines. For example, if my character is an 8-year-old girl, I make sure that I give her a name that was popular for baby girls born 8 years ago. I just input, "Popular names for girls, 2011". This is another sub-aspect of trending.

You may also go to Amazon.com and find trendy book subjects to write about. As long as you write original content, this is fair game. If you want a mass of readers, why wouldn't you tie-in trends or write about trendy subjects and topics?

I recall how, during the summer of 2017, fidget spinners were all the rave. In other words, they were on trend. They were billed as a potential comfort/focus toy, although teachers were not buying it. I thought about piggybacking off of this and writing a book titled, "Madison and her Fidget Spinners." I discovered that the name Madison was a popular name for girls in 2000 and used that name for my characters since teens were the ones with whom this toy was most popular. I believed that fidget spinners might evolve into a new twist by Christmas of the same year; so, I had a window of time to write this book. Unfortunately, I had a lot on my plate, so I did not get to capitalize off of this toy sensation.

You can also piggyback off of others' winning ideas. For example, when I was writing books about homelessness, I wrote one called, "Diary of a Homeless Frog." In this manner, I still wrote about my topic matter, but I wrote using the Diary concept that was made super popular by the books, "Diary of a Wimpy Kid" and whole series and movies that spawned from Jeff Kinney's genius.

The same librarian that I mentioned earlier also shared with me that The Mayor's Summer Reading Book Club in Dallas makes selections based upon popular books that children read. Just about every city has one, and it is worth your while to court libraries, donate your children's book to one or more branches and promote it heavily so that kids know about it before the summer comes. It is also important that librarians see, and can document, this high readership of your children's book. This could result in your book being placed on the Summer Reading Club list. In turn, this could increase the readership of your book, making it increasingly popular. Video is King!

Video is King!

Ideally you want your videos to be on a channel, requiring that people subscribe in order to have the best experience. Having this requirement affords you the opportunity to capture more emails, which then affords you opportunities to stay in touch with them through various other means.

Studies show that people tend to stay on pages where there is engaging video content. You can use such videos to share your story in snippets, give viewers insight into your book and other things you do (such as speaking engagements, blog posts, Periscope, etc.) Ensure that viewers can tell pretty quickly (early in the video message) that they stand to gain something by staying on the page to watch the video. This is often referred to as the take-away. You can even offer a special incentive to get them to watch the whole video. A message like, "Everyone who stays at the end of the video will find out how to get a free download of my eBook on (subject here) or my guidebook on (subject here). At the end, keep your promise and tell them where to click to get that free eBook/guidebook, or where to go to obtain it. Another reason you want people to stay on the page with your video for longer periods of time is your analytics look better, which, in turn, can help your placement on search engines.

By all means, do not think you have to be the only one making videos that help you with promoting your book.

Do not be afraid to ask visitors to your events, book signings, etc. to take videos and pictures and even selfies. Ask them to post it to their social media sites, or to send it to you for posting. If they post something directly, be sure to repost, like, share and comment.

Having some of your book's discussion, reflection and excerpts on video can also help your book become more mediagenic and reader-centric.

At the end of your videos, you can do either of the following to engage, capture and grow your viewing audiences:

- ✓ Post an attractive message that reads something like this: Please give us a thumbs up and subscribe. That helps us get visibility on YouTube (or Vimeo, etc.)"

- ✓ End your videos with a clip of yourself the way Steve Harvey does for The Steve Harvey Show; where he points out where people can subscribe to his YouTube channel and to the location where they can view more of his videos.

- ✓ Keep it simple by asking them for a Thumbs Up to show how favorable they thought your content to be.

The ideal is to get people to subscribe to your video channel, Patreon account, social media insiders, etc. so they can potentially become part of your tribe (more on that later), to get them to bring others along, and to improve your analytics (more on that later). Subscribers equal email contacts, a number which you will want to see grow on a continual basis.

A final suggestion for videos is that you have a book trailer video made. There are talented people on Fiverr.com who can create them for you for $5-10. You will need to provide them with a clear, concise brief where you describe what images and text you want on each panel (page). You will also want to attach any of your own images for them to use.

For the Audiobook

Look on Fiverr.com under audio and see who offers voice talent. Find ones with excellent reviews, experience on Fiverr and who can provide samples of similar work. Try them out on a $5-10 gig to see if they do well with a small portion of your book. For example, let them read the first chapter as a test of their abilities. If you like them (their voice, tone, volume, and pronunciations are spot-on), court them for a while and tell them about the vision for your book. When the book is fully proofread and copy edited, if you have found someone you like order the full gig from them but ask for two rounds of revisions to be written into the custom quote. If there are special pronunciations, send them the dictionary link where they can push the microphone to hear the proper pronunciation. Also be sure that after they deliver the final project, you submit your modification request in a timely fashion (usually under 3 days) but be thorough in proofreading and copyediting their work all the way through before closing out the gig. Mispronounced, slurred, or *missed* words should not be in your audiobook. So, always make sure you have exactly what you need (proper volume, etc.) before giving a review and closing the gig.

Book Covers and Book Cover Contests

In an ideal world, the cover designer you use would be able to read or carefully skim your book to get inspiration for the cover design. In the self-publishing world, which does not happen as often as it does with traditional publishers.

Write a design brief describing how you want your cover to look, including the spine, front and back. You may go to the library and bookstores and look at volumes and volumes of books on many shelves. Make note of what stands out, and this means literal notes with pad and pen. When I was in final stages of signing off on my book cover design, I was at a library and noticed that Sue Monk Kid's book, "The Secret Life of Bees," really stood out on the shelf of a multitude of books. This was because the spine was a bright, vibrant yellow. I had my designer change my spine cover to match this feature and it gave my book more pop.

I have been incredibly happy with book cover designs provided by 99Designs, Design Crowd, and Ashely Dowell, an illustrator and editor-in-chief for Dowell House Publishing. Check out their websites to see their platforms for designing book covers. Sign up to get on their email list because many periodically send you discount notifications for as much as $100 off.

If they ever offer a discount through an email, that might be an enjoyable time to order a book cover. While designing is taking place and designers are sending your ideas, ask your family, friends, and followers to tell you which designs they like and why. Post designs under consideration on your blog, social media, and website. You can also post polls where you invite people to give you feedback on your selected top favorite designs. Another simple technique is to email family and friends (and anyone else who you want to add) and get their opinions on the cover. I would suggest that you limit contests, polls, and emails for feedback to five designs at a time. It is quite possible that you will get a much higher number than that. I got a total of seventy-four designs for one book cover and 47 on another (although not all of them came to me at once). I would select my top five choices and then get opinions from that small set. Later on, a different permutation of my top five choices might be used to get feedback. I can share that in my contests I have normally had two designs that were almost neck-to-neck in my polls and surveys as well as my personal preferences. The winning design often won by just a slight margin.

Be sure that when you finish your contest and have a winning design, you request all of the files that you will need because once the handover process is done (with the wining designer getting the prize money and you getting your files) they have no further obligation to send you anything else. You can check with your printer or print-on-demand distributor, such as Ingram Sparks or Kindle Direct Publishing (KDP) to find out which file formats and types of files they need so you can ask for everything you need.

The beauty of some of these companies is that you pay your price upfront, and a portion of this will be handed over to the one winning designer out of the crowd of designers who elect to be a participant. Each graphic artist who responds favorably to your design brief and creates a cover for you will do so knowing they are competing with other designers with no promise that their entry(ies) will be the winner. This is a win for you because you get more designs to choose from; especially if you write a winning brief that is easy for them to understand. Some graphic artists will sit on the fence and wait for a while to see how the contest is going before they jump in the fray. Sometimes designs from late participants end up being the best of the bunch. I believe these late entrants may be the most competitive out of the group, and that they observe with an extremely critical and competitive eye while silently saying to themselves, "If I were in that contest, I would do xxx and not include xxx." In other words, they think they can do better – which is a bonus for you.

99Designs designers will make changes for you if you ask because they want to win. You can ask several designers at once to change something, such as their book cover color, the size of something, the spine, the fonts. If you like a particular cover in blue but want to see what it looks like in red, ask them. Trust me, they aim to please. If you think a particular design is too busy, ask them to eliminate some of the clutter. If you notice a special feedback comment is coming from your pollsters or other opinion sources, take that back to the designers and ask them to incorporate, eliminate and tweak accordingly.

The designers operate off of a code of conduct, and other designers who may or may not be a participant in your contest may point out violations. For example, my book was about a theme park setting, so one designer chose to put something like the title or my name on a ticket-like graphic. Since this was not specified in my design brief, and was an idea from a particular designer, I was not able to ask someone else whose cover I liked better to add the ticket concept to their design.

When the contest is drawing to an end and you have selected the winning design, the 99Designs team is getting ready to pay the winner. Before this happens, make sure you get everything you want and need from them, such as the right types of specific files in the right formats. For example, there might be an eBook version of the cover that has to be in ePub format and a print version that has to be PDF, JPEG, Mobi or some other format.(See eBook chapter for more information on eBook formats). All of this information will be based upon who you use, so refer back to Universe, Christian Book Publishing, Xulon, CreateSpace (or others) and get a list of all the files and file formats you need in order to publish your book in all the forms you want to publish it in (such as eBook, soft cover book, hard cover book). It is well-known that the more formats you offer, the more people you will reach, because different readers prefer different formats of books for distinct reasons. Archer likes hard-cover print books because he has a library with shelves and shelves of his favorite books. Amos likes eBooks because he travels a lot by airplane. Fiona likes audiobooks because she drives long distances to and from work. Greer likes audiobooks because she commutes by train. Quincy likes softcover print books because she or he likes to have something to hold in his or her hand – he/she loves the smell of the paper, and how it feels to turn a physical page.

Once the chosen designer hands off everything you request, they receive their contest winnings from 99Designs, and they might not help you after that. Even the 99Designs team will make you aware that you need to request everything you need before the entire contest is over. They use a countdown method and will wait for you to either communicate that you have everything or for the countdown clock to run out. Only then do they pay out or hand out the winning monies.

Fortunately for me, my first 99Designs designer (a guy all the way around the world in Romania) stayed in contact with me for as long as I stayed in contact with him. We connected on LinkedIn, and I sent him messages there and through email. He always responded. I had an incredibly positive experience with this individual.

I later did two other book covers through 99Designs and their contest platform. Believe it or not, I designed about 70% of the cover of the book you are currently reading using Canva Premium.

One website, Pickfu, allows you to test covers with the public by asking something along the lines of "Which potential book cover do you like best?" In fact, you can also use them to get feedback on book titles. It costs $20 to conduct a poll on this website, and some people consider it to be a worthwhile investment because there is merit to testing the market. That is why market companies, market testers and market research companies like Pickfu, The Media Panel, Integrated Research Associates, Inc., GRK, Capstone Research, etc. exist. No one, including you, wants to devote money, time, and energy to something that will fail in the real marketplace. Feedback, criticism, and kudos from potential customers is worth its weight in gold.

See link here: https://www.pickfu.com/books#utm_source=bryancollins&utm_campaign=partner&utm_medium=website

In addition to social media and other internet tools, you can go to places like the mall, trade shows, groups where you are affiliated (fraternities/sororities events, alumnus meetings, book club meetings, writing critique group meetings [even if you're not a member], libraries, bookstores, places where your book's target audience go, church groups/meetings/events and anywhere that you can legitimately present your book cover options and get feedback. Take your feedback seriously, including downright objections, and use it to tweak or change your tactics.

Without a discount, 99Designs can be expensive. I love them, though, and was able to afford to use them for a cover design for one of my books. In my opinion, it was the best cover design I have ever had.

An alternative, which is less expensive, is to have two different Fiverr designers design a cover and have a contest on your blog or social media to decide which one is best.

An even cheaper alternative is to design it yourself on Canva.com (not my personal recommendation as a sole option). You can use Canva to design flyers about your book as well. You DO want flyers.

Amazon also recently launched a book cover contest component. Do some research and see if what they offer works for you.

One more idea is to have people on your email contact list vote on your cover, summaries, and any other content where you are considering different options. Also add the options on your website and blog, send tweets with your cover designs and get votes that way too. Write a short keyword dense description in each place where you post your cover designs.

(I have a package where I help with book cover contests for just $15).

Note: You might also get information for cover designs by looking at covers designed by award-winning book jacket designer, Chip Kidd. He gave an interesting TEDTalk, and the video titled "Designing Books is no Laughing Matter. OK, it is." Among other things he said the cover designer distills the book's contents in picture form and serves as interpreter and translator.

Once you have a final cover design you can use it on your business cards, bookmarks (more about this later) and flyers. In addition, you can upload it to your Twitter page as a background. See link with instructions for accomplishing this at http://www.dummies.com/social-media/twitter/how-to-change-your-twitter-background/

Events, Curriculum and Books

Many notable authors have curriculum from which they birthed books or books where they created (or had someone to create) curriculum. I personally know many in the reference and self-help genre who have done this. In fact, curriculum, whether it came first or after the book, has helped many authors to sell more books.

Curriculum helps readers of your nonfiction book to have a deeper, richer reading experience. In addition, it gives them a chance to put into practice the principles and concepts that are covered in the book. This makes the reading experience more engaging.

There is merit to using curriculum in fiction books as well. One example is having readers compare and contrast characters in your book. You can also have a lesson where they compare and contrast characters in your book with character like Harry Potter, Katniss Everdeen (from Suzanne Collins' Hunger Games), Beatrice Prior (from Veronica Roth's Divergent series) and popular book characters; both young and old.

The main point is that curriculum should be related to the book and tied to the goals and objectives you set for the target audience. One simple curriculum or lesson plan that can accompany a book where you want readers to compare two things with a thorough and critical light is to have them use a Venn diagram to compare and contrast. A Venn diagram is made of two interlocking ovals, with room on each side for the distinctive features or characteristics of something to be listed and the things they share in common in the middle. Many worksheet templates of this graphic organizers can be found all over the internet.

To be creative and engage visual, tactile, kinesthetic learners, instead of sheets of paper you can do this activity with the Venn diagram consisting of two interlocking hoola hoops. I set them up and then had my students get on the floor and put sticky notes or index cards with the differences and similarities written on them in the appropriate spots. This trumped pencil or pens and worksheets with the Venn diagram on them.

At any rate, curriculum should be in every teacher's wheelhouse. To that end, if you cannot create the curriculum, perhaps you can hire a teacher, teacher candidate or retired teacher to do it.

One handy expandable lesson plan template that I like to use for lesson plans that cover 5 days looks like this:

Set Up					
Teacher/Author Action					
Student Action					
Materials/Supplies					

Group Arrangement					
Homework					
Test					

Of course, this is what I would use if I were doing an author visit or workshop with students, and wanted to include a lesson that will engage them in the book content using reading standards.

The set-up is your hook. It can be a video, an image, a quote; anything that quickly hooks them into the lesson.

The test can be done by having them write down one thing they learned which was often on index cards as a "ticket out the door," observing their product, worksheet, etc.; or it can be a quiz or formal test.

Authors are not the only ones who can create (or have someone create) curriculum for their books. When I worked as a reporter, I once covered a church where a retired curriculum specialist and others on her team developed curriculum for their summer Vacation Bible School using the popular book by Suzanne Collins, "The Hunger Games."

Looking back at the article that I wrote, the students were divided into twelve districts during the reaping (a term used in the book. It's also a harvest related biblical term). They had a victory obstacle Course, did camouflage activities, tunnel crawls, balance beam feats, weight-pulling, and more engaging activities during the week.

The students received survival packs during the VBS kickoff, and their hunger was modified to "hunger for the Lord." They also modified the catchphrase, "May the odds forever be in your favor," to "With Jesus, the odds are ever in your favor." This particular church had astonishing numbers of postings and links (video and others) on social media.

Just imagine what a writer of a book can do in terms of implementing curriculum with ingenuity like this, and having their affiliate or other groups implement the curriculum. Of course they would need to let the media know about it – because that is mediagenic.

Although the above section references curriculum, some of them featured events as well. Events can be a great platform to help authors like yourself with their book promotion platform. Plays, conferences, graduation ceremonies and other events are places where authors may be able to rent a table and pitch their book to attendees.

However, there is something even better than that – an author producing and hosting their own event. I know a lady who wrote her first book after she got out of prison. She used CreateSpace, an Amazon self-publishing arm, for her book. She then wrote a play about the book. When the play debuted, her book sales went through the roof. This mediagenic young lady told me this, "For the first time, I don't have to worry about how I'm going to pay my rent." She had such massive sales, that she won an Amazon contest where she got a $15,000 bonus on top of massive quarterly royalties. Amazon also offers a $50,000 Breakthrough Novel Award for their grand prize and four first place awards of $15,000.

Many pastors and church leaders host different conferences and sell massive quantities of books. Even those whose conference package price includes a book gets to count those book sales. As you can imagine, this dynamic puts into play maximum wisdom for moving high inventories of books.

BOOK CONTESTS

One great offering out there for writers of books of various genres is book contests. If your book wins an award, it is an announcement to readers that it has exceptional merit in the world of books. If the media, such as a newspaper, sponsors the award, that is all the better for you. Consider how The New York Times (a newspaper, aka the media) is the compiler of a bestseller book list. Do not think it is impossible for you to sell such a volume of books that you end up on that list. It could happen for you.

One non-media contest that I like that honors children's books, illustrators and authors is Moonbeams Children's Book Awards. They charge a fee of $95; but many contests assess reading fees and such. I would not let the fact that there is an entry fee deter me. I would do a cost-benefit analysis and weigh all factors.

See Moonbeam's link here: http://moonbeamawards.com/Moonbeam_Guidelines_2017.pdf

The Mount Everest of book awards for children is the Newberry Award, and its accompanying medal. It is an award in the literary arena based upon factors that distinguish the author for making a significant contribution to literature. Judges for this award review the books' theme, plot, setting, style, and character. What weighs heavily is how well your book is presented for an audience of children. You will notice the letters ALA in the URL. This is because The American Library Association (ALA) have a selection committee that judges books for this award.

See more details here: http://www.ala.org/alsc/awardsgrants/bookmedia/newberymedal/newberyterms/newberyterms

A similar children's book award is The Caldecott Medal given for picture books. This is also an ALA award.

See more details here: http://www.ala.org/alsc/awardsgrants/bookmedia/caldecottmedal/caldecottterms/caldecottterms

Ethnically-based awards can also be found in this arena. One notable award is The Coretta Scott King Book Award named in honor of the late wife of Dr. Martin Luther King Jr.

This award is for African American illustrators and authors in the young adult and children's genres. The books also must explore universal human values and African American culture.

More information available here: http://www.ala.org/rt/emiert/cskbookawards

In my state, The Texas Library Association gives a Bluebonnet Award for children's books of literary excellence. It is sponsored by Bound to Stay Bound, but the children do the voting. This leads me to conclude that you definitely want to get your books in school libraries if you covet this, or similar awards.

See more details here: http://www.txla.org/TBA

You might also wish to look into state-specific awards in the state where you live. If your state has a library association, this is a suitable place to start your search.

Different writer's leagues and associations that have other purposes and objectives also offer literary awards. In my state there is both the Texas Writers League and The Texas Association of Authors. They both charge a reading fee, and provide an award emblem for the winning books.

See their links below: http://www.writersleague.org/

https://books.txauthors.com/mobile/default.aspx

You should check to see if your state offers similar associations and leagues; and how you might enter your book into their award competitions.

Boston Globe, a Massachusetts newspaper, sponsors the Horn Book Award. There are other media-based book awards. For a list of them, visit this website: http://www.ala.org/alsc/awardsgrants/bookmedia

For other children's book awards, visit this website: http://www.underdown.org/childrens-book-awards.htm

You can get a Pulitzer Prize for your book if you meet certain criteria. This is another award for distinguished books, and it is awarded for a variety of genres. As you know, the Pulitzer Prize is given in categories other than books.

http://www.bookspot.com/awards/

Another category of prize, where the awards are given in literature and other areas, is The Nobel Prize. It has been given over one hundred times as of the writing of this book.

See more interesting details at the following link: https://www.nobelprize.org/nobel_prizes/literature/laureates/

I also like to use Writers Digest and Poets & Authors (also the name of a non-profit entity) magazines to find out about all kinds of writing contests. Note: They also take poetry and other submissions, according to their submission guidelines and they offer articles, webcasts, and other content specifically for authors and writers.

Writer's Digest is where I found out about **Inkkitt**, a company where terrific books and the power of readers can help some authors land book contracts. I am going to check them out further; but as of the publishing date of this book, I did not know a lot about them.

You can check them out on Facebook, or their link provided here: https://www.inkitt.com/

About Book Contests: With your goals of gaining media and readers that favorably respond to your book, you stand to benefit a whole lot by snagging a few awards. If this happens to you, be sure to write and distribute a press release about it and let me know.

Costumes, Parades & Mascots, Oh My!

A lot of organizations, such as The Boys & Girls Club, have Storybook Parades in place of Halloween celebrations. This type of event still gives children a chance to don costumes. They celebrate books and book characters through a day-long event. The children parade in book character costumes while holding their favorite book. Judges award prizes for several categories. In addition, the event features break-out sessions where the children meet with authors who showcase and discuss their books.

To double-dip in such events, you should consider having a costumed figure from your children's book. A fairy, a princess or another common figure are some ideas to start with. Children can easily pick up costumes at Halloween and costume stores. You can also originate a character and have the costume created, and then let children buy them directly from you or from your website. One way to promote the costume, character and book is to contact teachers. They may be able to have you come as a career day presenter in the author or writer (or costumer/seamstress) category. Other places include recreation centers, dance/martial arts studios, and daycare centers. If you contact Boys & Girls Clubs early enough, you may be able to be a book talk presenter during the breakout session AND have children parade in your costume while carrying your book for the parade. Of course, you would want to take plenty of pictures and videos and share them at the time through media such as Periscope and Facebook Live. You can also take a few moments to send social media posts during the event and invite others to do so. You can also send a press release and invite the media in advance.

One other photo Opp idea is to take pictures with the children who are wearing the costume and holding your book. I would suggest that you have their parents sign a permission form in advance; so, this might require some coordination with the organization leaders before the parade date.

Some clubs of this type might allow you to hold a similar event at their facilities, even if you organize it. Do not be afraid to ask. You might also wish to weigh whether giving away a couple of costumes might help you to gain more media attention, buzz, hype, and readers.

If you think costumes are just for children, consider how comic con, cosplay (costume play) and other events take place around the world and get adults involved in costuming. These partakers wear fashion items and costumes that represent a particular character. Perhaps your book might fit better in this universe if it is not a children's book.

***

When it comes to parades, I covered many of them while working as a reporter. I always saw many media personalities there. In fact, often the announcer was a member of the media. Christmas, Veteran's Day, Martin Luther King Jr's Holiday, Black History Month – these were all times when the city of my birth held parades.

As a reporter, I would often walk alongside the parade progression on side streets for a while where I could catch some of the crowd response and capture extra details such as a parade mascot that temporarily came apart from the float. I would then sprint to the balcony of a particular hotel overlooking the final parade route.

I have to tell you that, if I had seen anything newsworthy taking place on the side streets, I would have scooped up another story.

What I am saying is that, if you have a book with a tie-in to either of these events, you should seek to be a parade participant. Having a float with your costumed character (or mascot) is just one potential idea. All you have to do is find out who is coordinating the parade or look for the online event flyer. This is often where they accept applications for float and parade participants. You could even do an appearance in a costume with a wearable sandwich board A-frame board featuring your book cover.

Parades often come with ancillary events. Some examples include meetings/sing-alongs/rallies on the capitol steps, memorial events and food events, after parties, etc. On 9/11 of each year, many cities have firemen who do the symbolic march up the steps of their training facility in honor of the men and women who lost their lives serving on 09/01/01. Perhaps you can find a tie-in opportunity for such events and show up as an author. If nothing else, you can certainly share your information (card, etc.) with the media, and follow-up later.

The point here is that people (potential readers and the media) remember memorable, colorful, and engaging events. You want to be a part of as many high traffic events that are covered by the media as you can.

Just make sure that your target market of readers is also a factor that you consider.

***

If you are not sure a costume or costumed character works well with your book, consider having a mascot that represents the theme of your book. For example, a lady named Ms. Odds and Ends is the mascot derived from a character in a play that I wrote. Although this is not a book, it still carries the same concept. Ms. Mascot is to go with me when I do presentations to teens. These presentations are related to my 501c3; a homeless eradication non-profit that I run.

Mascots can represent ideas, concepts, and messages or embody characteristics to be used as an engaging piece to accompany your book. Imagine having your mascot show up for your media events, or dressing like the mascot yourself and showing up for an interview, at your book signing, etc.

***

For the Oh, My! Part, two extra book exposure opportunities that might work for children and youth are bookmarks and origami crafts events. If you play your cards right, you can contact libraries for Book Buddy or craft events and see if you can come as a featured craftsperson, who also has written a children's book. There may also be instances when adults would be interested in designing bookmarks.

One other idea is to have a bookmark design contest, where you provide handouts with a bookmark template on one side; measured at 4"x12" or 2"x6". You can also provide a means for people to download this template (highly recommended).

Your rules, a place for the person's contact details (such as email and phone number, school name, library, affiliate – how they found out about the contest) should be on the other side. You can notify teachers, librarians, book clubs and affiliates of your contest. You should set it up where the winning design will be used for your bookmark during promotions and fix it where you award a prize to the winner. This would mean that you will get an authorization from the winner, and that you have a disclaimer everywhere that you promote the contest.

The disclaimer can simply state that all submissions to the contest become your property.

You can make a big deal of this contest and provide a means for people to submit their entries, such as by mail and email. You also need to set a deadline for entries. When the winning design is selected, hopefully through polls and votes from your affiliates, social media connections, etc.; you should announce it in a big way.

I strongly suggest that you hand out these forms at any of your book events, trade shows, etc. and encourage people to submit entries.

One corner bookmark, pictured below, can be made with construction paper, regular and jagged scissors, and glue.

Material breakdown for this bookmark (per child) is as follows:

1. Main piece of construction measured at about 10"x10" (for main body)
2. Pink or red piece of construction the size of a sticky note (or you can use sticky notes of these colors)(for tongue)
3. 5"x1" white strip of construction paper (for teeth)

4. Two 2"x1" squares of white construction paper (for sclera - white part of eyes)

5. Two 1"x1" squares of yellow, pink, or blue construction paper (for the added fun color)

6. Black, blue, brown, or green markers (to color the iris of the eyes)

7. Construction glue

8. Regular scissors

9. Zig Zag cut scissors (arts/crafts or dressmaking)

This handy bookmark is superior to the long skinny ones, because it actually holds your place in the book.

Directions

Start by giving children a colorful piece of construction paper, measured at about 10"x10". They will later get white, yellow, and blue or black for the eyes, and red or pink for the tongue, along with white for the teeth. Put other colors aside.

Demonstrate to children how to diagonally fold their paper in half and make a crease. Wait until all have duplicated this action.

Demonstrate to children how to unfold this middle crease, and then take one corner and fold it upward so that it meets the middle of the creased line they just made. Wait until all have duplicated this action.

Next, demonstrate how to fold that middle crease again. Everyone should now have a double triangle (with the triangle's vertex facing downward) with one of them revealing the triangular flap they made when they folded one corner to the middle crease.

Demonstrate as you make an inward fold on both sides of that triangular flap. Wait until all have duplicated this action. Now there should be three triangles and the mouth.

Demonstrate how to fold the two corners down, on top of the original triangular flap. Wait until all have duplicated this action. Everyone should now have a triangular folded piece that looks like a kite.

Demonstrate how to glue the tongue on the bottom triangle, which is beneath the flap (or use sticky notes). Wait until all have duplicated this action.

Give each child their white squares and demonstrate how to cut ovals for the eyes. Wait until all have duplicated this action.

Give each child a yellow, pink, or blue piece of construction paper and demonstrate to them how to cut two smaller ovals and glue it to the bottom of the white pieces. Give each child a yellow, pink, or blue piece of construction paper and demonstrate to them how to cut two smaller ovals and glue it to the bottom of the white eye pieces.

Give each child a blue, black, or green piece of construction paper and demonstrate to them how to cut two smaller ovals and glue it to the bottom of the yellow/pink or blue pieces. Give each child a yellow, pink, or blue piece of construction paper and demonstrate to them how to cut two smaller ovals and glue it to the bottom of the white pieces. Or you can have them use markers to color the bottom portion of the irises.

Demonstrate how to glue each eye to the two sides of the flap overlooking their original flap. Wait until all have duplicated this action.

Give each child the white strip and demonstrate how to make a jagged cut along one side. Wait until all have duplicated this action.

Demonstrate how to glue this across the two sides with the eyes (underneath) so that it goes all the way across. Cut any excess. Wait until all have duplicated this action.

Have them each write their names on the back of the bookmark.

Let bookmarks dry thoroughly, and then put to use.

While these are drying, you can read them your delightful book.

Note: If you had trouble with these directions, a YouTube video tutorial for a very similar bookmark can be found at https://www.youtube.com/watch?v=gXhOQTlr6K4&app=desktop

About Amazon Author Central

Amazon's Author Central is an excellent place to help your book to be more discoverable, get exposure, increase your ranking, and keep track of your sales and post winning content. Setting up your account on Amazon Author Central is easy. You have the power to input and update content as you see fit. For example, they have an Author Page where millions of potential readers can find out more about you and your writing. You will have an exclusive direct link (URL) for you and your book(s), which is an excellent asset. Using this URL, you can also post to Facebook, Twitter, and add it to your email signature (Where people who get your emails will receive the active link as a signature feature – this will augment your marketing efforts). You can put your biography, photographs, blog posts, videos, information about your tour events, and other relevant information on your personal Author Page, and update it as you see fit. I strongly recommend that you add video reviews to your page, as I have explained that video is an excellent marketing tool (see chapter titled Video is King).

They recently added a feature called Amazon Author Insights where you will find a suite of useful utensils and services. It is also there that you can gain more insight into how to make your eBook (Kindle) more prominent. Kindle Scout can enable you to reach readers and whet their appetite for your book before it comes out. Note: Kindle Scout is different from Kindle Direct Publishing (KDP), but both are excellent to get to know better if you are a serious author.

I highly recommended that you sign up for their KDP Newsletter, enroll in their Search Inside the Book feature and reach out to Amazon Support to get author help from their highly skilled staff. If/when you get a website, be certain to add a link to Amazon's Author Pages on that website. This will enable people to easily travel directly from your website to your Amazon Author Pages. In addition, you will get updates and notices. I received a notice about their Kindle Storyteller Contest, where they offered a $20,000 cash prize.

See link to Amazon Author Central here: https://authorcentral.amazon.com

Email List Building

At events for your non-profit (if this applies to you) or as an author of books; have a sign-up sheet where people can give you their name, email, and social media handles. Keep building the list. You can use Constant Contact, Mail Chimp, or a similar service to reach these people with periodic updates and announcements about your book, the contests, and the launch date and book signings. Be sure email campaigns target only the appropriate people, and that you do not use too many images in your messages.

Some authors also send physical or digital newsletters to people on their email contact list. You have great flexibility in what you want as your newsletter content.

One thing that I strongly suggest is that you send snippets from your book in many of your newsletters and other emails. Be sure to give away other useful information. Aim for about eight emails about your book. On about ¼ of them, provide links to sites where your book can be reviewed and purchased, and directly ask the recipients to buy your book. You can also embed your video link into some of your content. On all of your emails, ask recipients to share the content with others who they think would appreciate it.

If you view the sample email contact list under Your Book Signing, Your Table, you will see one column dedicated to social media handles. You will want to use this information and reach out and share something with people who give you their handles within a week's time. Seek to establish a connection (a relationship) over time. From the column dedicated to Reading sites, you should use that information to reach out to places where they are active and see if they have reviewed and recommended books. If they show a pattern of leaving positive reviews with 3-5 stars, you might wish to ask them if they are interested in reading and posting a review of your book on that site.

You will also want to give people choices about how often, and what kinds of emails they want to get from you.

Marketing Tools

One superb marketing tool to have is a URL or link. If you have a website, a link to your book(s), etc., your unique URL can make you easier to discover and distinguish among all the other options out there. If you do not know how to generate a URL, I have provided the steps below. In my example, I am using an existing Power Point Presentation.

How to turn a Power Point Presentation file into a Flipping Book and then a URL

Here are the steps:

Convert your finished PPP file into a PDF using a PDF converter app or website like Convertio.

Save the PDF under your documents, drive, PC, or flash drive. Be sure to remember where you save it and under what name.

Go to a search bar where internet users input their queries and enter https://www.flippingbook.com Online.

In the upper left, in green is a rectangle that says, UPLOAD PDF

Click on it and it will enable you to find your PDF file under your file Documents, drive, PC, or flash drive.

Click on the proper file.

Click OPEN when the proper file name shows in the rectangular space next to FILE NAME at the bottom.

Flipping Book will show you a message in the upper left corner indicating that it is uploading PDF. At the bottom will be a message that says that it fill convert your file to a Flipping Book once it is loaded. Under that message, the file will show a status of "loading." When it is loaded, the file name will appear at the bottom.

Once it is finished loading, it will show a thumbnail of the file and the file name in blue on flippingbooks.com. The page count will then appear on the left.

To the right of this is an option menu. Click SHARE (in most instances), although EMBED might apply, depending on what you are doing. I will not go into it here, but I encourage you to look into it more deeply on your own.

You will see a Flipbook Link with a URL assigned to the flipbook.

From there you can either copy the link (to paste it elsewhere), or create a QR code, or share directly with Facebook, Twitter or

If you choose to generate a QR code here (I will explain another way to do so in this chapter) click Generate Code. Using a toggle bar, you can increase the size or reduce the size of the QR code generated, and you can download the QR code as well.

Making a trackable link is another option if you wish to explore this and what it includes. I will not go into it here except to say it gives you a chance to track traffic, but I encourage you to look into it more deeply on your own.

One excellent marketing tool to have is a QR code that is specifically for one of your projects. It could be for a book, a media kit, a website, or something else. They are useful for enabling people who you have or want to attract to your book where they can order it, to your website for different purposes, to your digital storefront like Etsy or TeachersPayTeachers and more.

Steps to make a QR code from a URL

Go to the QR code app on your phone.

Click on the icon at the bottom that looks like a QR code.

You will see the word Creator.

Click the plus sign on the upper left.

Under the creator Search Bar enter the website URL

Click Create on the upper right.

2 QR codes will appear.

Click on one of them and then click Save on upper right corner.

After you save it, click the download icon on the upper right and you can save to history or save the QR code.

Use the QR code you generated on digital media such as flyers, brochures, one-pagers, media kits, press release; and on other marketing items such as t-shirts.

Free eBooks with different content can be offered for those who purchase your main book. This distinguishes from the eBook version of your main book. For example, for the purchase of "Write a Mediagenic, Reader-Centric Book," I also offer a smaller eBook with additional information for authors. Often the way it works is that the buyer gets an eBook download link in their email. When they click on it, they go to a place where they input which email, they want the download link sent to. Once they input the information, a direct download link is sent to the designated email. I know this seems like extra steps, but this is often how I see it done. Technical talent can usually do this for you.

My research shows me that you can have eBooks as stand-alone books also, and there is a wealth of websites out there where you can feature them. I also have discovered that, even if you have your eBook on CreateSpace, you can also have the eBook version of it elsewhere. If you want to price your eBook where you can gain the highest royalty percentage on CreateSpace, price it between $2.99 and $7.99.

* People can sometimes obtain no-cost Adobe Reader to read an eBook in PDF format. For ePub books, there is more universal use; where someone who has a smartphone, tablet, e-reader and computer to read the book. EPub means electronic publishing. Any file with an .epub extension is in this format. It is more universal than Mobi.

Mobi is used by Amazon for Kindle readers. It is a Mobipocket file which can be used in low bandwidth devices. Kindles and some smartphones can be used to read files with the.mobi extension.

eBooks can be made available in ePub, PDF and Mobi format.

Some authors run short-term promotions to rack up reviews by offering their eBook for $0 on a temporary basis. Some sites limit how low a price you can post. Smashwords Store is an excellent place to initiate this. If Amazon discovers that the same book offered on their site is free elsewhere, they will drop the price of your eBook to $0 on their site as well. Keep in mind that there are no royalties paid out for free eBooks, and that this strategy helps with obtaining review, as well as increasing readership. After your promotion is over, you can raise the price everywhere where you feature your book for *sale*.

Consider putting your eBook on FeedBooks (feedbooks.com) and ManyBooks (manybooks.net). They will give you more exposure.

You can even apply to be featured on ManyBooks during special book promotions and launches for just $29. They have almost 400,000 readers.

Other book promo sites I like are as follows:

Booksandthebear.com is highly active on Twitter. Sometimes they discount their intensive book promotion package and lower the price from $299 to $99. This promotion lasts four weeks. If you are doing other things to promote your book, this could be an excellent complement to consider. They also have a $10 social media promotion that is catered to your book based upon checking out what it is about. Either way they promise an audience of over 200,000.

ReadersGazette.com is a place for indie authors to get exposure. They also publish book news. I have noticed that they have some great summaries for the books that they offer on this site.

BookGoodies.com often runs free Kindle eBook promotions for a few days at a time and you can temporarily highlight your book as a giveaway for the short-term. You can also submit an author interview to this site.

On Fiverr.com, there are some sellers who have a whole slew of followers on social media, and they offer to blast those followers with your book information. Check them out under the category Digital Marketing, subcategory Social Media Marketing and click on Shoutouts & Promotions OR look under category Digital Marketing, subcategory Influencer Marketing and look at the various offers to promote your book on their websites, blogs, podcast, radio show, etc.

Online book club https://forums.onlinebookclub.org/viewtopic.php?f=83&t=42908

Blog book tours are not really a promo site, but a new means for doing blog book tours without leaving home. It involves scheduling interaction using your blog and those of others who you have vetted and reached out to in advance. They typically will have a blog of a similar nature or topic to your book. It is a promising idea to get a list of such blogs together while working on your book. I have done guest posts and received guest posts in the past, although I did not do it as part of a blog book tour. Please research this exciting way to interact with readers and get to know others in the blogosphere!

***

I have heard a lot of authors say that they have been told by numerous people that they went online and ordered the eBook, yet they never received royalties for those "purchases." This means that the person who said they ordered the eBook online could be telling a falsehood, or the online stores are not properly disbursing royalties.

In order to prevent this, and to have more control over your own eBook sales, you may be able to purchase Dropcards. I ordered some from a writer's group with which I had a membership, the Texas Association of Authors. Furthermore, because of this membership, I had an opportunity to rent a table at the Texas Book Festival and sell my book in 2013. I had a perfect bound copy available for viewing and handling, but it was not yet perfected enough for me to sell (it was close). However, through Dropcards I was able to sell eBook download cards. I even sold these cards at the Laundromat, at the gas station and other locations long after the festival was over.

Please see the article that I wrote about Dropcards, along with pictures.

Dropcards: What Are They?

According to http://www.dropcards.com/learnmore/, Dropcards is the leading provider of mix download card solutions for the industry of recreation or amusement. Musicians, music studios, Fortune 500 companies, movie studios and authors use them to sell access to their creative products. When I saw the use of one demonstrated, I noticed that Dropcards allow the buyer straightforward digital access to the product. I call them the digital download card.

In business since 2004, Dropcards boasts themselves as leaders of the download card market.

As an author, I have begun to use them to provide buyers access to my new eBook. I was skeptical at first, but my mind is now at ease.

Dropcards: Reasons to Use Them

There are many reasons to use Dropcards. If you are an artist (musician or author), they can be another revenue stream for you to use to sell your product to the public. One advantage that B. Alan Bourgeois pointed out when I spoke to him about the Dropcard feature available to author members on his website (www.txauthors.com) is that they increase sales for the author, because people can buy the Dropcard, on the spot (also referred to as point-of-sale). As the founder of Texas Association of Authors (TAA) pointed out, often people will forget or neglect to order an eBook later, if they encounter the author at a festival or other event. Dropcards are a win-win for the buyer and seller; also known in this case as the reader and author.

I agree, as I found that as long as I have been letting people know that I have been blessed to have my book available as an eBook, I've have only shown one indication (financial) that they actually ordered the eBook at a later date.

However, in late October when my eBook release of "Xtreme Ride Wish: An Untwinnable Day," took place, I sold my first several copies of the eBook by selling the customer a Dropcard at the end of my pitch. The first couple of sales were at the Texas Book Festival, where I had a space at the TAA table.

The Dropcard has a website featuring the sponsoring company's name as an extension of the Dropcard website. Customers who purchase a Dropcard go to that site, enter their email address, and then input the unique access code assigned to the card. One extra nugget of advice that Bourgeois gave is that the seller should identify the name of their book on the card so that the buyer remembers when they get to the site and see offerings of several authors.

Another bonus to the buyer is the ease of using them. They do not have to have an account; they are generally able to complete their transaction in under a minute.

My Dropcard Experience

In addition to the Texas Book Festival, I attended a Release Your Greatness event the following Saturday. Customers who I talked to wanted to purchase the Dropcard, or seriously considered doing so. I explained it in an easy fashion since they really are super easy for the customer.

When you give away a free eBook for those who sign up for some offer, set things up where they can go to your website and fill in a contact form. From that you can send them an email with instructions for downloading the book. Be sure to send some type of thank you letter along these lines.

Dear Reader,

Thanks for signing up for my bonus online eBook. It is my hope that you will be glad you made this investment of a few minutes in order to obtain it. I have poured everything I know about writing and self-publishing into the main book How to Write a Mediagenic, Reader-centric Book), as well as what I know as a former member of the media. It took me 21 years to accumulate the knowledge in my mediagenic book and this bonus book, so I believe you will be in great shape by getting access to it in one fell swoop. In addition, this accompanying eBook has bonus material not found in the main book, but which is relevant for authors of fiction and non-fiction books Most of the bonus material was also included in my curriculum at a couple of Dallas area community colleges where I taught a class titled, "Writing Children's Literature That Pops, Dazzles and Sells."

Some of the bonus content is basic, some of it is practical and some of it is only plain fun things to know. Either way, with both the main book and this eBook, you should be able to go far in your dreams to become an author.

Since my specialty is self-publishing, I do not have a lot to offer in regard to getting book deals within either book. However, I do have that knowledge, and can transfer it to you. I can even guide you in writing a query or a book proposal. I have my own book consultancy company – Writezous Publishing/Writezous Works.

One vendor on Amazon (who was not selling a book) added a free eBook about eyebrow shaping to any orders for their special brand of tweezers. Tie-ins of this sort make sense. An author of a self-help book about finances can offer a free eBook on budgeting, or an eBook with different simple forms and spreadsheets with instructions for filling them out.

Another way that an eBook can work for you is if you have a means for those who buy or download it for free to find out about your related workshop or similar event. For instance, because my book is for authors and about writing, I might have information about an upcoming writing workshop that each person who gets the eBook finds out about when they download it.

Book Launch Tribe

A book launch tribe is your exclusive group of vetted individuals who you will single out to receive restricted access to some goodies in exchange for providing a review of your book when it launches. I suggest that, once you figure out the ideal time to launch your book, before it is printed, that you seek a tribe. One lady I know, who wrote a book about relationships and launched it on Valentine's Day. If you have a Christmas book, the holiday season is an excellent time to launch it. Give some thought to timing and calendar tie-ins when deciding on a book launch date. What you are doing here is taking something that is already on people's minds and advising that you have a book which covers or addresses that content in some way. There is a reason books about former presidents tend to come out during election time. There is a reason books (even older ones) about Alexander Hamilton became popular when the hit biographical musical show about him became a sensation. What this should hint at is if your book has been available for a while, and some related sensational product or production hits; you need to re-promote your book. This should include updating/tweaking all digital content so that it is keyword dense.

There is a reason bullying books flooded the market when the nation started paying more attention to bullying prevention, how cyberbullying has entered our environment and how many lost their lives due to bullying.

Be time-minded and season-minded. It will pay great dividends in terms of increased sales, buzz, and hype.

You would typically give the tribe access to things like your manuscript/advance copy/book, any special newsletter/blog/Periscope, digital images for which you hold the copyright and other content; along with whatever you want to give to them in exchange for being a tribe participant. Some authors give their tribes copies of their previous books or the manuscripts, a special and exclusive email where they can contact them, notices of interviews they will conduct, a book tour schedule or other incentives that make the tribe feel special, hand-picked, and vitally connected.

In exchange, you will want the tribe member to provide book reviews on sites like Amazon.com, Goodreads, Barnes & Nobles, Smashwords, Jacketflap, etc. You will want the major portion of those reviews to happen when you first launch the book. Be sure to provide them with the direct/full URLs, so they can post directly to the site where your book is located.

All that activity will spawn more activity. You can recruit these tribe members on various platforms; but for purposes of brevity, this will address Facebook.

On Facebook you will simply announce that you are accepting applications to be on your book launch tribe, and then provide an active link where they can go from there to your Google Doc application. Do not engage in SPAM or anything that violates the platform's policy. It is important to set an application deadline, and to make sure you time this to give yourself time to select your tribe members, provide them with the manuscript/advance copy/book, and to give them time to read the book before it officially launches. You will screen the applications, paying special attention to their response as to why they believe they will be an ideal candidate for your tribe. For example, if your book is a Christian book, you will not want atheists or Moslems in your particular tribe. If your book is about a vegan lifestyle, you will not want committed carnivores. You get the picture.

You will use tribe member's emails for most of your content, so be sure you have a place on your Google Doc for them to give you this information. Of course, you will interact with them on Facebook (or other social media sites), as well.

When giving tribe members a chance to read your book, you will also provide them with tailored social media posts to post once the book comes out. Consider reading the book, "Jab, Jab, Jab, Right Hook," written by Gary Vaynerchuk or at read the chapters where he addresses Facebook and any social media sites where you have a presence. Use that knowledge to post information about your book on social media. Secondly, it will help if you know a little bit about Search Engine Optimization and keywords. The more you know about these two things, the more impactful and effective your posts can be.

***

Book Launch Application example. You can use Google Docs or a similar app to create a fillable PDF of your Tribe Member Application.

Exclusive Invitation-Only Book-Launch-Tribe Application

I am offering an invitation-only book marketing and promotion plan that I have elected to share with you and a few others. It is set up for the launch of my forthcoming book, "Write a Mediagenic, Reader-Centric Book." I am so ecstatic to have reached this juncture of the process and elated to extend to you an opportunity to be an exclusive participant in my tribe. I am seeking sold out participants to help me before, during and briefly after the launch of the book. Part of my strategy is to give the hand-picked tribe members exclusive social media updates/blog posts/newsletter content, Periscope exclusives, copies of a former book (to be provided later) and more. If selected, you will receive these things in exchange for assisting me during launch week by sharing updates/posts (some of which I provide) on social media, leaving reviews on Amazon or another site of my choosing and sharing content on your website, blog, and other connections. You will do this and receive a few bonuses, as follows:

1. A free advance copy of my book in eBook form or manuscript form
2. A peek at what is going on behind the scenes with this book
3. A few secret tips on how to make your own book mediagenic – one that the media will love!
4. Digital images for which I own the copyright
5. Other digital downloads that I own

I can only afford to offer this opportunity to totally committed people who will read the book and perform the agree-upon actions when requested. This form is designed so I can find the perfect tribe candidates. That is why I will look at all application submissions with an extremely critical eye. Everyone who makes the cut will be notified by email invitation by the end of (insert date here).

* Required

Top of Form

How and when did you first hear about "Write a Mediagenic, Reader-Centric Book" *

Tell us why you would be an invaluable member of the Book Launch Team. *

Feel free to be as detailed as you would like - this is the question we will be paying closest attention to. :)

Please link to your blog and/or social media page(s) *

It is okay if you do not have a blog or formal "business" pages. Feel free to link to whatever best represents the platforms you will be using to share updates about the book launch. :)

Have you made a purchase on Amazon.com within the last year? If so, do you remember your log-in information or have the capacity to recover it?

Are you an Amazon Prime member?

Do you have a profile with a picture of yourself on any book sites like Goodreads?

Are you a published author? If so, is your book posted on Amazon.com? Please share the title here _____. **

Is there anything else you would like to add?

Your Full Name *

Your Email Address *

Your mailing Address

Check this box to acknowledge that by submitting your answers above you have read and understand that this would be a volunteer role for a limited time, in exchange for specified free products and services provided by the "Write a Mediagenic, Reader-Centric Book" launch tribe. *

- Yes, I totally understand and agree. I am on board
- No. Thanks. Not at this time

Please provide a secondary email address if you have one:

_____

Thanks for applying,

Shirley A. Hammond and the, "Write Like a Reader, Think Like the Media," Book Launch Team

**Note: You will want this information because Amazon does not allow authors to publish reviews of other author's books. This does not mean that you will automatically eliminate authors from your tribe; you just might ask them to post their review on Barnes & Nobles, Goodreads, Jacketflap, GoRead or another site where it will benefit you the most.

If you are inclined to have people sign a non-disclosure agreement where they commit to not sharing your book contents for a period of time, Rocket Lawyer and other sites offer this service, sometimes with a free trial period.

The agreement often includes a clear definition of what confidential means and specifies that the tribe member does not disclose or modify for their own use the document that you specify. You will need their mailing address (on the tribe application) so it can be input in the binding agreement. Online sites like Rocket Lawyer will enable you to send the document to the person's email for them to sign, date and return. You will then sign where designated.

Getting Reviews

You have already seen newly launched books which already have scores of reviews on sites like Amazon.com. You have probably even seen some books with reviews printed on the back cover. If you have ever wondered how this could be, some of the secrets are shared in this chapter. Read on.

Earlier you were advised of the multitude of benefits found in using videos across several platforms. One winning idea is to have a few people do their reviews on video. Make sure it is of high quality, that their voice volume is sufficient, their appearance is appropriate for the book and audience, and that they properly hold the book or a prop that represents it during the taping of the video. You may be able to find people on Fiverr.com to do video reviews. It may cost $5-$10 dollars.

Many times, you will be able to send the reviewers a PDF copy of your manuscript, as opposed to a printed book. The advantage of sending a manuscript is that it is ready before the final book and they have more time to read and send you a video before the book launches, so that you have a video review to post during the launch or preliminary stages of your book release. The advantage of sending a print book or advance copy is that they can show it in the video.

Fiver.com's talent along these lines may be listed under the category Video and the subcategory Human Billboard or something similar. One video review short that I like is on a book mentioned already under the chapter on book summaries. The video reviewer is down-to-earth, gives a compelling review and ends by summing it up that he gives the book 5 stars and then provides his contact information. This all gives the review and the book credibility.

Please see link to this video review; which is posted directly to the Amazon Author Central page: https://www.amazon.com/gp/customer-reviews/R9M1DHH2X66KP?reftag=va_cr_lb

While we are at it, please take a look at two reader reviews that were posted on Amazon.com for one of my books, "Christmas Plus: Delightful."

#1 I enjoyed this book so much! It is as though the author has shared every experience in her life in a heartfelt, compassionate, entertaining, and uplifting way. I highly recommend it to everyone!

This anonymous review was posted recently with a verified purchase.

#2 Christmas Fun for the Whole Family

By Stephan on March 17, 2011

Shirley Ann Franklin's CHRISTMAS PLUS is a wonderful book composed of ten Christmas-themed short stories and two longer stories. The book's primary target audience is children, however it also includes stories that will appeal to readers of all ages.

CHRISTMAS PLUS has everything from stories that appeal to the sense of imagination, such as "Daniel's Musical Pajamas" (a tale of a little boy who discovers his musical talents through the instrument pictures that magically play on his pajamas), to stories that teach children the virtues of kindness and giving, such as "A Chunk of Christmas Pie" (a tale of a woman who shares pie with a homeless man and is blessed for it). There are even stories that address the topic of ethnic minorities discovering the value in their cultural heritage, such as "Mei Ling's Christmas Pajamas" and "The Christmas Stockings". The short stories are all wholesome and written in realistic voices that children can relate to. The dialogue is smooth throughout, the vivid imagery and sensory details accentuate the settings, and the characters are well-rounded and interesting to learn about.

Additionally, there are a handful of stories that would intrigue adults. Franklin tackles an array of issues from a grandmother dealing with the hardships of the economy during the holiday season ("The Christmas Biscuits") to a young wife/mother who discovers how to handle the struggles of marriage ("The Christmas Courage"), to an elderly couple enjoying an intimate moment ("The Christmas Smooch"). Indeed Franklin displays her versatility in writing material from diverse perspectives all across the age spectrum. Her stories reflect not only the idealism and goodwill associated with the Christmas season, but also the sometimes harsh reality of trying to make ends meet in a bustling time of year.

To sweeten the deal, she includes two full length stories ("The Magnificient, Marvelous Ferris Wheel Daze" and "Memoirs Of An Antique Doll") that are extremely creative and imaginative, and remind one of the works of great Children's Fiction writers like Roald Dahl and Lewis Carroll. I guarantee your children will be entertained by these tales, but at the same time they will be enriched intellectually. For instance, Franklin often uses higher level vocabulary terms and offers the definition in the same sentence. She is clearly a writer who has an appreciation for the duality between making great art and producing material with an educational slant.

I highly recommend CHRISTMAS PLUS for anybody looking for a nice gift for their children, or even for adults who are looking for something to read that will put them in a cheerful and positive mood.

***

Professional Reviews: Besides individuals, it is great to get library, school, and other professionals to review your book. A professional review is slightly different from a reader review in that it is based upon a more detached objective expert opinion that comments on the quality of the book. Some which you may wish to court includes the following:

Kirkus Reviews and Booklist are two options. Do your research and see if you are interested in what they offer.

Library Journal is a journal used by many public librarians. It is these same individuals who sometimes post reviews.

BookPage is also a book review journal. There are all kinds of articles and book reviews in this publication. I talked to a public branch librarian who personally told me that the main library in Dallas (Acquisitions Department) often orders for the branches based, both upon the recommendations of librarians and publications like this. I have even known many librarians who have written children's books, and they understand the advantage of being featured in these publications.

Newspapers: See if your daily or weekly newspaper will post a book review in their Arts and Lifestyle (or similar) section.

School LIBRARY Journal is a journal that many librarians use in order to decide which books to order for their inventory. Because of this, it is a promising idea to at least try to have your book reviewed in there. Other than getting a bonafide librarian to review your book and submit it to them, there are a few more requirements. It should be easy to find online or a copy of the journal, which you can obtain at a library.

HORN book is another notable industry publication where delightful book reviews can help authors. You should also look into getting a review in that publication.

Sometimes these professional publications want a copy of your book or manuscript well in advance of publication (as much as four months), so start your research and begin your process with them early.

Your Goal and Why

According to Book promotion guru Steve Harrison, your goal is to sell 1,000 books in the first 90 days. People who do so typically sell tens of thousands (or more) of copies in the first year. Harrison has several special program offerings for authors; including one called Quantum Leap. If I had the funds, I would invest in it.

Two more things:

1. SPEAKING ENGAGEMENTS

Do not overlook speaking as a means to get exposure and sell your books. Speaking can put you in front of readers and enable you to make a connection. Being thusly connected, can make people more likely to buy your book afterward. I have seen it happen.

I went to an event where one author/speaker had written a book about his grandmother's wit. He had a half mannequin dressed in a scarf and a dress while he talked about his book and read excerpts. After the event, he and all authors presented their books for sale at tables in the foyer. His line was the longest, and I attributed it to his use of a prop, his storytelling aspects and his high engagement and connection with the audience during his speech.

Consider becoming a member of an organization where you can develop your speaking skills, such as Toastmasters. Also consider joining a speaker's platform where you can advertise yourself as an SME speaker. One of them is GigMasters. In the video universe there is also TEDTalk; which is a platform for SMEs to share their area of expertise, comedy routine, etc. before live audiences, and later on videos. You can view video clips and read the transcripts directly on the site. Many TEDTalk authors have also written books, which are also available on the site.

It is important to seek to connect with your audience and tell your story during times before a live video audience. Once again, as I said in the Mediagenic segment, I highly recommend that you read the book by storytelling entrepreneur, Gary Vaynerchuk. Once you have identified the right story to share, practice it often before delivering it publicly.

2. LIBRARIES

Also look into joining libraries as a Friend (i.e., Friends of the Dallas Public Library). This gives you closer connections to libraries, library staff and readers. You will be on their mailing list, where you can receive notices of events and other information. This could be a gateway to schedule a library book signing. Along with this you should consider joining writers groups and writing critique groups that are often held at libraries and bookstores. You might also check to see if your library has a patron pick and library reads programs, which consist of books recommended by the respective populations. There are also library scavenger hunts. One library in my area had a half sheet with fourteen blank lines. The children were to discover some fun trivia about buildings of interest. Posters of fourteen such buildings were found all over the library. Children were to fill the half-sheet out and turn it in.

During the final stages of publishing, the author decided the change the term Mediagenic to Media Magnetic. You will see this in the title, cover and other mattter, but mediagenic will still show up in other places. In addition, this book was originally written in 2016, so you will see references to CreateSpace, which is now Kindle Direct Publishing (KDP).

Bibliography

1. Evans Hurst, Chrystal, "She's Still There: Rescuing the Girl in You," Zondervan Publishing, 2017 2. Vaynerchuk, Gary, "Jab, Jab, Jab, Right Hook," HarperCollins Publishers, 2013.

www.ingramcontent.com/pod-product-compliance
Lightning Source LLC
Chambersburg PA
CBHW031426290426
44110CB00011B/543